THE SOUND
OF SILENCE

THE SOUND
OF SILENCE

Lois Fiedler

FLEMING H. REVELL COMPANY
WESTWOOD, NEW JERSEY

To Tom and Louise Fry,
whose faith has been like a beacon,
and whose kindness and understanding
have meant so much to so many.

I

THE SOUND
OF SILENCE

. . . through a dark valley

I HAVE WALKED through a valley darker than Death's,
Entered alone, except for the companionship
Of complete despair and loneliness—
I could not see where to place my feet,
And stood still lest I fall into a pit.

My voice cried out to God in pain.
He came, and showed Himself and His love to me,
He led me through a dark valley
To the other side.

You—standing in a dark valley,
Knowing the agony of its pain—
I hold out to you the goodness, the sweetness
And the strength
Of God.

I CREPT, filled with fear, along a wall that was
Cold, dark, wet from my tears
And covered with shadows.
Alone, I clung to the wall,
This endless wall of despair and rejection—
It was all I knew.
What made me turn my eyes
To see light at the edge of the shadows?
What made me raise my hands,
Asking for strength and help?
What made me strain to my feet
To take a step toward the light?
One step, another—slowly—
Quickly now, hurrying toward the brightness.
The beautiful, blinding, blessed Light
That makes truth so clear,
Life so full and free,
A straight path on which to set my feet.
I look again to the shadows
And see clinging to their walls
Others, crying to be free of them,
Yet afraid to leave.
I call, I beckon and I would share,
For now I know the Source
Who gave the light, the truth and the
      straight path,
And I hurry, for I am eager
To be enfolded in His love.

CAN YOU *see it?*
The vast, black upon black void,
So empty, so very much of nothingness,
And yet so final.
The tiny figure standing, helpless and blind
In its darkness.

Can you feel it?
The agony, the wrenching and rending
Of the heart and mind,
The despair and utter aloneness.
See the watchful eyes,
And the tender hands of friends waiting
To catch and lift if there be need.

And now a shaft of Light,
Solid, straight and true,
Cuts through the black
And rests on the figure.
The figure stands—so very small—
Eyes closed, head up and hands clenched,
Weary, bruised, but standing,
Gathering strength and sureness
In the Light.

The figure moves and the Light moves with it,
Always strong and bright,
Showing the way.
The watchful eyes smile,
The waiting hands relax,
For now the need is less.

IN MY BEING is great darkness,
I cannot see beyond.
I long for peace
And despair sits close at hand.
My heart seeks joy
And knows only its own unshed tears.
My ears strain for harmony
And hear instead my own strident discord.
My body stumbles in weariness
And yet does not sleep.

O, Lord, let Your presence light my soul
And Your peace send despair running.
Cleanse me and make me like crystal
That my heart might know You and so joy,
That my ears hear notes of beauty from within,
That my body might find rest and thus serve well.

May these blessings shine,
Reflecting Your love.

O, LORD,
Take this cup from me!
Its taste is of bitterness and gall
And it causes such pain.
Like a poison it eats.
I cannot sleep and my eyes blur,
My heart lies heavy and would stop.

Stretch out Thy strong arm and
Undo the cause of my grief;
Yet, I pray, rescue my enemy
That he may not see the lowest part of hell.

Be gracious unto one who loves Thee,
Grant me Thy mercy,
For I am guilty of wrongdoing
And seek Thy forgiveness.

Thou art God of all
Yet Thou art my God,
Strong in might,
Tender in forgiveness,
Gentle in love.

DEAR LORD—

Thou hast given me talents which I have used,
And in their using I achieved something.
My pride rides high, for I have done something well.
I have left something permanent of myself in the world,
And my joy and satisfaction in my own ability are great.

A small moment of glory was mine,
And when I looked to share it I found no one but myself.
There was no loved one to claim me,
To have pride in me
Or in what I have done.

Dear God, what is success if it is for myself!

My loneliness is greater than my life.
There is no one who can share as I need to share.
I am alone—
Aloneness is nothingness, and nothingness is agony.

But in the midst of this great fist, this coil of pain,
I remember who gave the life and talents, the mind.
My pride crumbles, Thou art very near,
And I give thanks to Thee for Thine unspeakable gift.

Give me strength once more to stand alone—
To hold my head high—
To keep my eyes clear and on Thee—
To accept humbly any honor given.

16

Wilt Thou accept me graciously, then, and in love—
    I have no other place to turn—
And use me as Thou wouldst.

                                        Amen.

MY DEAR GOD—
Why is man?
Why did You make him?
Why am I here?
What is my purpose?
Why life?
Who and what am I?

I care desperately,
        But for what and why?
What was is not
        And what is will not be.

I looked into myself,
        And found nothing.
I wept in agony,
        And no tears came.

Who is accepted and rejected?
What is there of man to accept or reject?
Why this mind,
This body?
Is there to be no peace
In my life?
Where do I go?
Then what?

Will You answer?

LORD—

I'm ready,
Why aren't You?
Please get on my schedule
And don't keep me waiting!
Everywhere I turn—
There stands a wall.
Sometimes a door opens.
Won't You open them all—now!
Waiting is hard, Lord.
When will You do things my way
Instead of my doing them Yours?
Your way is best, I know,
And You work all things for good,
But
Waiting is hard, Lord.

HOLDING THE HAND of one whom I loved,
I walked down a path
Smooth from being trod many times,
And so dear and familiar to my feet
That I closed my eyes for a moment
And walked blindly,
Letting myself be led by my love.
While my eyes were closed
My hand was released.
Stumbling, I fell.

When I opened my eyes my love was gone
And there was darkness no light could penetrate.
Helpless, I tried to rise,
But had neither strength nor desire
To lift the burden of my woe alone.
How long I lay there, writhing,
Moaning in my anguish—

I heard a gentle Voice
And saw a soft light.
I waited and listened and watched,
And the Voice became a command,
And the light became blinding,
And I was running with outstretched arms
Toward it—to the top of the high mountain.
There I found green pastures,
And still waters,
And Love that restored without end.

Now I walk a path with many stones,
But my hand is held by a Love
That will not release
Nor ever let me fall.

SHALL I GO, LORD?

Let me place my hand in Yours
With the full faith and sure knowledge
You will guide me and not lose me.

Stay close by and see me
Through days of uncertainty,
New people, a new place,
That I may do my work well and without fear.

Use me here, Lord, if You can.
Let myself be put aside
That You may be seen,
And not the other way around.

Let me do well, Lord,
Not for me, but for
You.

I have found my Lord!

HOW can I tell,
    how can I describe
The wonder of it all!
The joyful abandonment of a child
    at play—
The leap of the heart at the coming
    of a new Love—
The calm quietness of a summer day
    at noon—
The eagerness of the mind in search
    of knowledge—
The driving force of vitality
    unknown before—
The urgency of trying to
    catch up—
The excitement of being
    one's self—
The utter humility of losing
    one's self completely—
All of this—and so much more—
    is mine.

I have found my Lord!

O GOD, how strong Thou art!
Like a bird held captive in a gentle hand
I fought to free myself from Thee.
My soul cried out in agony against Thee
And what Thou wouldst ask of me—
It was too much.
I could not see Thee, for my eyes
Were filled with tears,
And my heart with night.
Inside I screamed but my lips were sealed
And no sound was heard.

Thou didst hold me fast,
And in great love,
Until my tears were gone
And the night from my heart.
My weary soul said, "I yield,"
And Thou didst give me peace.

With the new day my soul could say,
"Behold, the very goodness of God
Covers you as the grass the field,
As the sky the earth.
He is there in the midst of your war,
To heal your wounds and see you safely home.
Follow Him."

O LORD, when I think upon Thee
My heart is so full of joy it must break
And my mind so overwhelmed with Thy greatness—
My whole being so filled with the glory of Thee,
I want to sing,
To run,
To laugh.
I know a gladness,
Joy,
And happiness
From being extended beyond myself
And stretching to reach Thee.
What delight is mine in giving myself to Thee,
And in the giving to know I receive
Ten thousandfold from Thee.
I drink from Thy cup of love
And ask for more.
Thou great good Giver of all gifts—
So dear,
What can I offer in return
For Thy love for me?
The least is myself, yet that
Is what Thou wouldst ask,
And so I give
Willingly, gratefully and with thanksgiving.

O GOD—
How wondrously great You are!
To know
>You really can fill all my needs;
>That I am able to depend only on You
>And that I am capable of it;
>The invigorating strength and life this knowledge brings;
>That, with You standing by, my feet are touching ground
>And that I can stand solidly;
>That, with You leading the way, I can walk
>In a straight path and not falter.

My life with You as full partner has just begun.
I sought Your comfort and You gave it freely,
And now I seek Your guidance in living,
Knowing if only I listen,
You will make Yourself known.

THE CLEANSING, scouring, scrubbing anger
At one's own self,
And the rooting out of the
Muddy bed of self-sorrow and pity;
The final full realization
That my life can be lived only by me
With strength sought and gained from God
And His love given through Christ;
That I am newly born in Christ
By commitment to Him as I am able;
The knowledge that future disappointments
Can be faced without fear;
That I am accepted more than rejected by others;
That I can enjoy life as well as find joy in it
And the responsibilities living brings—

All serve to help me know life is
    God's gift to me
And that He expects me to live it
    in and for Him
In the best way I am able.

How good to feel alive while glad to be!

🌹 29

DEAR LORD—
Thank You for a good stiff dose of indignation,
And for directing it at myself for a change.
Thank You for the chance to play the role
Of Camille for a while,
And then the eye-opening experience of laughing at myself
For prolonging its exquisite agony.
Thank You for waiting me out
Until the miseries went away,
And for Your loving care while
They were here.
Thank You for everyone who held my hand anyway,
While they were wishing I'd hurry up
And get back to normal.
And thank You for life—
Complete with its disappointments and problems,
And for Your love, mercy and blessings
Which let me face them.

Amen.

HOW GREAT has been God's force
In my life!
I came to Him, alone, adrift
In a sea of human-made problems,
Weary beyond measure and heart-broken.
In my darkness I turned to Him
And found light.
Days and months have passed
And as I have learned to know Him
And love Him—
Each day more than yesterday—
I have not found Him wanting.
He is the Answer—
There is no other—
And I commit myself and my life
To Him,
Knowing a joy and peace
Which words cannot tell.

GOD has seen me through dark times,
Their very blackness committing me to Him,
For I could not face them alone by my own strength.
So glad to cast my problems and heaviness on Him;
So freely and lovingly He came,
And my joy was like wine in its headiness.
The times of darkness are over now
And the joy has become deeper and quieter,
Bringing peace and confidence,
And the sure knowledge God will not loose His hand
That holds me.
I must use the abilities God has given me
To live my life as He would have me.
And yet so silently, so often
Does my own self take over
And I am caught in a web of my own weaving.
What brings me back?
    The simple beauty of communion—
    A look of displeasure from a friend—
    The knowledge I have willingly hurt someone—
    My own bewilderment.
Step by step (some leaps of joy,
Some painful and rebellious with feet dragging)
Do I grow in the knowledge and love
Of my Lord,
Knowing in Him only can true Life be found.

LORD—
Let me look ahead,
Not pressing, not pushing,
Not planning too rigidly,
But using each day as a part
Of the brick and mortar of the
Life I would build
With You as the foundation
And basic ingredient of the material.

Let me have sense enough
To let You help me build
And move me in completely.
Then, be my honored and deeply loved Guest
Who will live with me in the house
You helped to build.

Let it be a house of beauty
So that others will ask,
"Who designed it?"
"Who is your source of supply?"

And I can introduce them to my Architect and Builder
That they might build houses
Of their own.
                                        Amen.

Accept me, dear Lord ...

DEAR GOD—
Never let me be so satisfied with myself and my life
That I become a blank sheet of paper with nothing on it.
I know that my life is good because it is
A gift from You.
Make me aware that my brain, its knowledge and ability,
My body and its health,
My mind and its health,
All have been given to me by You.
Am I proud to have committed my life to You?
Where is my humility?
Can You still be seen in me, or have I put a cover over You?—
A cover made from the satisfaction gained from decisions
I have rightly made but which were rightly made
Because of You in my life
And not just because of me.
I say that I have completely dedicated myself to You,
But a look at myself makes me know I have not.
Being so human, so fallible, I may never
Be able to completely dedicate myself,
For my pride and humanness are ever with me.
Accept me, dear Lord, for what I am
And the little of me that I really do commit;
And hold me fast while I try
To give up the rest of me to You.
                                   Amen.

37

DEAR LORD—
I come to Thee now,
Asking what Thou wouldst
Have me do with my life.
Will I ever know again
The richness of life shared
Between a man and a woman?
If not, fill my heart with Thine
Abiding love and share all my days.
Will I know once more
The strength given and received in loving arms?
If not, give me Thy strength
That I may stand alone.
When the feeling of being suspended and dangling
Threatens my well-being,
Let me remember that Thou
Art always there with arms held out
To set me on solid ground.
May my faith in Thee never weaken,
For Thou art the foundation
On which I have been building
A whole new life,
And outside Thee I have no life.

Thou art my Lord, my Master and my God.
                                        Amen.

IT REALLY DOESN'T MATTER,
    does it, Lord,
Whether I'm smart or stupid,
    strong or weak?
To each of us You have given
A measure of intelligence and talent
Along with the gift of life,
And it's what we do with what we
    have received—
This is the thing that matters.
Help us to make it count
For something worthwhile.

You alone know my heart as I
    approach You
In a humbleness not known before,
And I ask that You receive this
    life of mine,
For I would give it all to You now.

39

WHAT lies ahead?
So much time left
    without a charted course.
A new life, painfully born,
Each day bringing its challenge
Of being lived in a new way.
No one to share—
    Conversation, children,
    Books, records,
    Meals, a joke.

A lonely time, but a rich one—
    A time to share with my Master,
    A time to learn of Him and to accept Him;
    A time to ask His help in decisions;
    A time to pray and to meditate;
    A time to praise and share His goodness.

What lies ahead?
So much time—so much time,
But not enough to do all the things
I could and would do
As my Lord would have me.

DEAR LORD, I would ask You to accept the labors
    of my hands
As well as the labors of my mind,
For I know the pleasure of digging in spring soil
And sifting the dirt through my fingers;
Of planting and watering and trimming and clipping;
Of watching plants sprout and grow;
Of walking behind a lawn mower and watching the cut
    grass fly
And smelling of its sweetness.
I know the satisfaction of kneading dough with fingers
    and fists;
And the good smell of bread and sweet things baking
    in the oven.
I know the unmatched satisfaction of seeing and smelling
A clean wash blowing and drying on the line;
And the crisp odor of a white shirt being ironed;
I know the incredulity of seeing dust return to surfaces
That I have only a few minutes ago cleaned,
And of sand and mud tracked in on a freshly vacuumed
    carpet
By the feet of children.
What can compare with a hot cup of coffee
Shared at the kitchen table with a friend or neighbor,
And the sense of weariness in the evening
After a day of sound physical labor?
For all these labors of love which Thou hast given to me,
I give Thee heartfelt thanks. Amen.

DEAR LORD—
At times I seem to be so busy praying
That I don't take time to hear Your answers.
And then I seem to be so busy with
Running a house, going to work,
Raising children, doing my little chores,
That I forget to pray at all.
How is it, when I want so much
For me to live in You
And You to live in me,
That I am such a mass of contradictions?

But in the midst of my all-or-nothing,
I would remember to thank You
For a healthy body and mind,
Normal children and the richness
They give to my life;
A comfortable home and good neighbors,
Friends who have stood the test of time,
And, most of all, for Yourself and
The fact that You hear my prayers,
Answering according to my need and
According to Your will, not mine.

Amen.

DEAR CHRIST,
In Thee have I found perfection.
My humanness and ignorance
Have let me test Thy greatness,
And I have not found Thee wanting.
Knowing Thee as I do now,
There is no need to test,
For I know Thou art all things—
Perfectly and flawlessly so.
May I not be found wanting
In my belief and faith in Thee
When others would test me,
Or if Thou would.
Let my mind, my heart, my life
Be directed in a straight line toward Thee,
Without a waver, or bend, or hyphen.
Let no obstacle make me stumble
Or change my path.
It is a long journey from me to Thee,
But knowing Thou art always there
Watching, waiting, urging, calling—
I place one foot before the other,
Head held high, eyes bright with anticipation
And arms opened wide to embrace
Thy great goodness.

Father, help me to learn ...

DEAR LORD—

I cannot see Thee
Yet I see Thy beauty all about me;
I know Thy presence and it is
Precious beyond all measure;
I feel Thy love and its warmth;
I am forgiven by Thee and marvel at Thy mercy;
I know Thy strength and the courage it gives.

I can claim Thee and all Thy greatness
For my own if I will,
And I do.
Thou canst claim me and all my smallness,
And do.

I should not ask for more
(But I will because I am human).

O GOD, I have asked Thee for so much
And Thou hast always given,
Knowing that I will keep asking
Because I am human and my need of Thee is so great.
I would ask Thee now
To make me know humility,
For I cannot be wholly acceptable
Until I am truly humble in Thine eyes.
I have found it so much easier
To love Thee than to be humble
For Thee,
And my pride for myself and
The things that I do
(Even when for Thee)
Is forever with me.
Wilt Thou tear this pride from me, I pray,
And then accept me as Thy humble servant.

Amen.

FATHER,
Help me to learn to forgive
As I am forgiven—
Completely and without question.
Forgiveness is sought in so many ways
And often without words.
I have asked and received without words,
And ask Thy grace to do the same for others.

Help me to be the stopping point for hurt
And not give back in kind.
Rather, ask forgiveness for
Giving others any cause to strike out.

Wilt Thou untie the knots of self-importance
That I might fall, straight and true,
As a plumb line for Thee—
Showing the way to the power, strength,
Gentleness, understanding, concern and love
That comes to me only when I place
Thee above me.

Amen.

DEAR LORD,

When I would covet what others have,
    turn my eyes to You.
When I would act against Your will,
    make my will weaker than Yours.
When I stand tall in pride and conceit,
    humble me.
When I would speak unkindly,
    cover my mouth.
When my mind knows dark thoughts,
    send Your light.

Let me so give my life to Your care
That it will be lived responsibly and with purpose.
Whatever I do, be it small or large,
Let it be done through You, in You,
For You.

                                    Amen.

DEAR GOD—
Thou hast heaped honor
    upon honor
And gift upon gift
    upon me,
When I am so undeserving.
I stand in awe and
    amazement
At Thy kindness and goodness.
May I glory in them for
    one small moment,
And then gently and
    carefully
Put them away in their
    proper places
That they be kept safe
    from harm and abuse—
Knowing that they are there
For me to draw on and to give
    in return when needed.
And then, surrounded by these gifts—
So precious, so rare, so treasured,
    so loved—
May I turn with joy and
    thanksgiving
To see Thee, and Thee alone,
As the focus of my life.

                    Amen.

LET ME be flexible, Lord.
In my honesty
Don't let me be so stiff-necked
That the neck will break when bowing.
Help me not to be rude
And not to strike out in frustration
When I am thwarted,
For my desire is not to hurt others.
Let me see the good I can do
Wherever I might be put,
And then do it as well as I know how.
Give me patience and understanding—
Above all, love,
So I may do the things I would rather not
With a good will.
Guide my mind and my heart
That they may stay centered on Thee.
Guard my tongue that it may not hurt.
Keep my hands off things
I should leave to others.
Let me always remember that
I am Thy servant and no other,
And should and would wait only on Thee.
                                    Amen.

O LORD—
Let the troubled waters of mind and heart be still
That I may reflect Thee.
I am so full of my own thoughts and wishes
Which can spoil and defame,
And I thank Thee for loving me when I am unlovable.
In the very depths of me Thou dost live
And I know Thou art there.
Why, then, do I so often cover Thee up with myself?
Give me the grace to want to do what I ought to do,
Let me follow the straight line of truth
    without hesitation,
Let me be gentle that I may not
    cause hurt,
Let me be strong that I might follow Thee
    wherever Thou wouldst go,
Make me humble that I might be emptied
    of self,
Let me know love for others as I
    am loved.
Free me, bind me, seal me for Thine own
And use me as Thou wouldst.

                                 Amen.

O GOD, Thou hast consumed my impurities
    in a white fire,
And tempered my soul with a steady
    heat.
Thou hast lanced my heart so the hurt can
    leave.
Thou hast cast me down so I may know
    humbleness.
Thou hast poured me from myself.
Then Thou didst come and give me
    life-giving warmth.
Thou hast healed my heart and
It beats steady and strong
    for Thee.
Thou hast lifted me and in my humility
I stand tall and straight for Thee.
Thou hast filled me with
Thy deep and always-present love.
Thou hast made me whole—
And caught me captive forever.

DEAR LORD—
It's good that You know all things,
For I can never say in words
How deep is my gratitude for
The love I know You hold for me
(Especially Your care in dark times).
My heart and soul are so aware
Of Your presence in my life,
And of the hope and joy,
Peace, comfort, courage, strength and life
Such knowledge brings.

How very glad I am to know You!

Yet, in the days that are ahead
(As in the past),
There will be times when I will
Forget these things
And even You.
Will You remind me then of Yourself
And bring me back,
For while loving You has not made life easy
It has made it worthwhile,
And I long to love and serve You well.
                                    Amen.

When memories and
loneliness crowd in . . .

A CLEAR CRISP FALL DAY—
   (Remember raking the leaves
   And sharing a laughing glance
   As the children tossed their small bodies
   Into the heap of your endeavors.)
A windy, sleety winter's night—
   (Remember the sudden shiver
   And the warmth of an arm placed
   Around your shoulder,
   The contentment of lying arm in arm
   Before an open fire.)
A damp-warm spring morning—
   (Remember the good smell of earth
   Freshly turned
   And the feeling of the world starting
   Life all over again.)
A hot summer afternoon—
   (Remember a leisurely drive,
   Or sitting under the trees, holding hands,
   Resting in a cool breeze.)

When memories and loneliness crowd in,
And my eyes sting and throat aches
From unshed tears,
Dear Lord, let me remember
Your love knows no season
And that I have joy, warmth, life and rest
All complete in You.

IN THOSE VERY SMALL HOURS
    of the day
When the night is nearly done
But the day has not yet made
    itself known,
Unable to sleep after awakened
By the cries of a small boy
    having bad dreams,
I stole from the house
To sit under the low-hanging
Branches of the trees.
There, in the quiet and peace
    of the night
With gentle dogs lying at my feet
    keeping watch,
My thoughts turned to my Lord
    Christ.
My mind fingered over the past days
And the blank stone walls which
    had met me
Wherever I seemed to turn,
And how each turn had made me
Still more dependent on Him,
Binding me ever more surely,
Ever more closely.
And I knew a joy and gladness
For His constancy and never-failing
    love.
As so many times before and as
Will be done again and again,

I committed myself to His care
and sought His guidance,
That my thoughts and actions
might please Him.

How good to be in God's hands.

LORD—
At the end of the day
My thoughts dwell on You
And how I found You brand new
    again this morning.
While I am pleased with myself
    for such discovery,
I know too that today I have probably
    Been the cause of hurt to someone,
    Unintentionally and intentionally,
And I earnestly ask Your forgiveness.

Let me love You as I should,
Using the gifts of life You have so generously
    given me—
That I might receive You
And then reflect You.

In following You
I know the challenge a child
    knows
When trying to place his feet
In his father's footprints,
And the delight that comes
With occasional success.
I walk confidently,
Knowing Your footprints
Fall on a sure path
Whichever direction You would have me go.

If I will follow.

O LORD, I know I have been truly blessed by Thee.
I have known the joy and beauty of loving Thee
And being loved by Thee in return.
Why then, this night, does my heart
Know such anguish, such sorrow,
Such loneliness, such despair?
Thou alone dost know their depths.
I would tonight nearly wish that
I had not given my life to Thee
So that I might tear it from my own body
And so be rid of it once and for all.
But it is not mine to take.

Grant me peace,
Surround me with Thy love and mercy,
Be very gracious unto me,
Give me strength that I might have
The courage to live for Thee
As well as the wish to die in Thee.
And please, dear Lord,
Be very close to me this night.

Amen.

DEAR FATHER,

As I kneel now beside my bed, I bring to Thee
    a problem
As yet unknown, for my heart is still full of one
Who is no longer here.
Wilt Thou start preparing me now to meet it
    unafraid and confident
When it does come, as I know it must.
When my body feels so strongly that it
    must be yielded to,
Wilt Thou take my hands and unclench the fists
    they will make;
Wilt Thou so fill my mind and heart that there
    will be room
For nothing except Thy fulfilling love;
Wilt Thou slow the restless legs and feet
As they stride about trying to make me tired
    enough to sleep soundly;
Wilt Thou give me tender mercy as I whisper,
    "Oh, God! Why?"
And turn my face resolutely away from anything
I might do or think that would be displeasing
    to Thee,
For my true delight is in pleasing Thee.
Grant me now Thy love and peace,
That my body may be kept and remain
Pure and acceptable and a living sacrifice
    to Thee.

                          Amen.

O GOD, when the day ends and darkness comes,
And I know with certainty that I won't be
        hearing footsteps on the walk
Or the front door opening with a "Hi!"
That I won't be folded 'round with strong arms
        and warmly kissed;
When I sit alone with my thoughts and longings
        and yearnings,
And when the tears start to come—for the nights
        are hardest of all—
May I remember to turn full face to Thee
And know the comfort, strength, joy and peace
Of Thy love for those who hurt so much.
When I go to bed, let me sleep secure in
        the knowledge that Thou art awake, always
        watching and always caring,
Always ready to take my hurt for Thyself in
        exchange for a deep abiding love that heals.
When I wake in the morning, may I be secure
        in the knowledge that my work will be done
        as well as I can do it, and done for Thee,
And that during that day, something will happen
        to make me laugh and know that life
        is good after all—that when dark comes again,
        I will know I am not really alone, for
        Thou art always there.
Help me not to let my earthly loneliness make me
        short-tempered with the children;
Don't let me hug my hurts to myself and spend
        my hours licking my wounds,

But let me enjoy the companionship of small
    boys whom I love and who love me,
Of good books that stimulate the mind and heart,
Of music that can enrich and soothe,
Of friends who care and are interested in me
    and the things that interest me
And for whom I care and am interested in.
For I do truly know the joy and happiness,
The concern and suffering for others that are mine,
Because I know and love Thee and am trying to
    give my life to Thee.
I know that Thou wilt accept it all if I can let
    go enough to give it.

DEAR LORD,
The tears still will come,
The heart still will ache
And long for a tender glance
And a strong hand placed over mine.
How long, Lord—
How long will this part of me
Be empty and make me know such loneliness?
Will it never end?
I know that You are watching and caring;
That Your heart aches because mine does;
That because of You I can stand and not fall;
That my joy is in sharing You,
And my knowledge of and love for You,
With others—
That they may know You too
And the very goodness of You.
Give me Your tenderness, Lord,
Place Your strong hand over my heart
And seal it for Your own.
Let Your face shine upon me
And fill my dark corners with light.
Let me be what I am and can be—
Let it be for You.

Amen.

DEAR LORD,
So quickly, so unexpectedly, so strongly, so insistently
Does my body make its demand.
May I acknowledge this need for what it is
And then seek from Thee the strength
To cope and channel,
That I may not abuse my body or profane it.
How is it, this desire, which is one
To be shared, but shared in love
And in the bounds of marriage,
Should pull so strongly now
That my eyes are turned from Thee for a moment.
To yield would mean such loss—
Self-respect, integrity, my commitment to Thee—

And yet I hear its song and feel its force.

Wilt Thou stay close by,
Let me be very aware of Thy nearness
And of Thine unlimited grace, goodness and understanding
For one who would but dare not
Let go of Thy strong hand
Lest I fall.

                                        Amen.

DEAR GOD,

When my body trembles
    from weariness
And the buffeting of facing
The world alone,
Brace me once more with
    Your strength;
When my heart aches
    and yearns
For the solace and comfort
Of loving arms,
Encircle me and enfold me with
    Your love;
When my mind thrashes about
    in confusion,
Give me wisdom and clarity
    of thought,
To know Your will and then
    do it.

Guide my right hand,
My left arm;
Show my eyes the road
On which to set my feet,
And then walk with me
With Your strength,
Your love,
Your will.

                        Amen.

IF I FORGET THEE, O Lord,
Forget Thou not me,
For I lose sight of Thee
    so many times
In so many ways.
Not because Thou art not
    there
But because I am blinded to
    all
But myself.

Wilt Thou then call to me
That I might once more
Hear and see Thee clearly.
                Amen.

DEAR LORD,
How far from You did I go?
Not far, yet it seemed a
    long way.
And now I seek You again,
Knowing the greatness and
    goodness
Of You—
The patient waiting and
    forgiving love.
Once more I know the joy
    of finding You
And letting You into my heart
    and life.

My need—so much greater;
Discipline—more willingly applied;
Life—more new and more responsible;
Joy—with more serenity;
Love—deeper, fuller, more fulfilling.

You have set me free from myself
    still another time,
Turned my eyes away from myself
To You,
And I see—more than before—
Your beauty and loveliness.

I am content.
                Amen.

I stand alone

I HAVE LOST a way of life
That suited me, I thought.
I was a wife and mother—happily so.
A mother now, but no longer a wife—
I have lost much.

What have I gained?

A life forever lost to the love of Christ
And being accepted and loved by Him,
Freedom and courage
To be a part of this world while yet
        apart from it,
To love any and all as God would
        have me,
To discover and then to be myself,
To have direction and purpose,
To have abounding energy,
To have emotional and physical health,
To have calmness and peace in heart and mind,
To have no fear,
To give of myself in love and concern
And to receive it as well.

A way of life has been lost,
But the joy in the new,
The challenge, the responsibility—
I stand, looking at its brightness and promise,
And know I can never turn back.

Will you come with me?

75

THE HOURS PASS so quickly
And a day is finished.
The days race by and a
Week has come to an end.
Hours, days, weeks, months—
Years—
All pass so quickly when I am trying
    to serve my Lord.
I wish there were more time so that
I could do more and serve Him better.
Maybe then I could walk and not run,
And give more quality to the quantity.
Why do I make such haste?
I know there will be others after me
Who will do more and do it better.
And yet I must hurry,
For so much time has passed
Before I could serve Him willingly
And with a whole heart.
Don't stop me—
There is so much yet I must do.

DEAR LORD—
Do You smile (or shed a tear)
When You see me
Looking at the world
As if it were made especially for me
And that only I can conquer it
With only my own ability?
What must You think!

How large the world is—
How small I am!

Peel the scales of my own importance
From my eyes
That once more I may see You clearly.
For only then will I be big enough
To know the world is Yours, not mine,
And if I am to conquer any of it,
It will be not by my own ability alone
But through You in love and understanding,
Strength and truth.

I LOOKED within myself today
And felt so infinitesimally small,
So very expendable and
Of so very little real worth
To anyone
Except my God.

To be so small and still so great
Is overwhelming.
It leaves me nothing
But to serve the One who loves me
          most,
For we will give ourselves gladly
To Someone who loves us
And for whom we can work.

I stand alone, accepted yet rejected
By my fellow humans,
And know, as every man must know,
          some day,
That I am loved and of worth
For what I truly am
Only by my God.

MY LORD dost know
The depths and the heights of me.
He knowest the narrow and the wide.

I am a motley one made up of
    good,
    evil,
    wise,
    foolish,
    strong,
    weak,
    tender,
    harsh ways.

And yet my Lord dost love me.
    This I know.
Nowhere can I hide, nor do I want,
    For I am His.

He knowest the secret places of me
And He fills them with His light.
He hath claimed me, marked me, set me,
Making glad my life.

I STAND ALONE,
Even though there are many people about me.
And I can,
Because my Lord is beside me
And God surrounds me
With His strength and love.

When hours of darkness and shadow come,
If I wait and am still,
I can feel the presence of my Master
Close at hand and know
He will guide me through them.

A peace fills my heart
And stills my churning mind—
So full of doubts and questions.
A strength is given that lets me stand erect
And look at the world
With eyes unafraid.

I stand alone,
And I can,
Because my Lord is beside me
And God surrounds me
With His strength and love.

OH, GOD,

How often are You regarded
As an eternal Christmas tree—
Being presented with want lists,
Offering gifts which are received
As if they were our due and expected
    as if our right!

You have given life itself
    in the beginning,
And redeem it when we ask
After abusing and wasting it.

You have given us minds
    and graciously
Allowed freedom to choose how
    to use them.

You have put us in bodies
    wondrously made
And turned them over to us
As instruments and tools.

You have given us tongues
Which we too often wag at
    both ends
Saying nothing or worse than nothing.

You have given us hearts
With which to love,
But with which we sometimes
       dislike or hate.

You have given us souls
To nurture and care for,
But which we neglect so easily.

You have given us Christ
To minister to our needs
And save us from ourselves,
Whom we ignore so well.

Thou great giver of gifts!
Will we forever receive and not
       give in return!

May we so love you that
       Our minds choose Your way;
       Our bodies honor You;
       Our tongues praise You;
       Our hearts love You best of all;
       Our souls are committed to You;
       Our total selves find in Christ
       A living Lord and way of life;
       Our lives are witnesses to Your glory.
                              Amen.

...let me be used!

O LORD—

Having been so bound up
In myself of late,
I forgot to be concerned
About anyone else.

Let me give love now
Where there is torment and anger;
Comfort where there is
Burden and bewilderment;
Help me to give freely of myself
If there be need or want.

Let there be no saving
Of me for myself,
Nor keeping of accounts,
For my own account with You
Should have been overdrawn
        long ago.

But You never left me
With insufficient funds
To cover my needs.

I can never repay,
Which leaves nothing to do
But use what You
Have given so generously.

May I use it well.

                              Amen.

                              85

IT IS VERY EARLY in the day
And I am up,
Eager for the day to begin.
How will God use me today?

Two small boys stagger into the kitchen,
Eyes still full of sleep—
Let me be a good mother.
I walk into my office,
Ready for a busy day—
Let me do my work well.
People will see me
And talk with me—
Let them see God in me.
I will hear and talk with men of God—
Let my knowledge of God increase.
Maybe I will be with someone who suffers—
Let me be concerned, love them and be a friend.

Let me be used . . . let me be used!

O LORD, USE ME—make me a sounding board, a mirror,
    a calm pool
In which others can see Thee.
Let those who knew me before I knew Thee
Know me now, and see plainly the difference.
Let them see the freedom that is mine through Thee—
Freedom from fear of anything of man;
Freedom from being bound to myself;
Freedom to have courage to do the things Thou wouldst have
    me do;
Freedom to love anyone, with a love that is free;
Freedom to be myself because I am in Thee.
May they see Thee in me, and know that Thou art good,
    because of what has happened to me.
May they see what a vital force Thou art—
The endless energy, the constant source of strength,
The calmness and serenity,
The ability to laugh at oneself,
The fullness of life,
The joy of losing pride and gaining humility,
The goodness of being alive because one is
    dead to himself
And has come to live in Thee.
Without Thee I am nothing.
With Thee I can do anything Thou wouldst have me do,
For Thou art truly my Master and Saviour.
                             Amen.

O LORD, I was a field, small, dry, parched and ugly,
Unused, not wanted, useless except for borning a crop
    of weeds
And an occasional good plant.
Then, consumed by a fire of loss and grief almost unbearable,
I was stripped bare of all things.
I lay fallow, scorched to nothingness, and
Those who saw me had no hopes of anything ever finding life
    here again.
Then from Your kind strong hands
Life-giving water was poured in gentle fashion—
Small amounts at first,
And then as I received the life-giving liquid
You increased it to a flood, and I was laid
Open, and the furrows from the swift-moving waters
Received their first seeds of Your love and goodness.
Now I am a field again—but with the desire
    and hope
Of becoming a garden full of good plants
That are nourished and tended by Your loving care.
May my prayer be that others may feed upon the plants
    which I bear
And so taste and take their fill of Thee
And know the feeling of a hunger completely satisfied.
                                                    Amen.

O LORD, I SEE THEE in so many places—
I look at the sky and see Thy serenity
In the white-mare's-tail clouds drifting;
I look at the trees budding in spring
And see my love for Thee as a small leaf
That will finally unfold to fullness;
I feel a soft wind blow cleanly on my face
And remember Thy Holy Spirit that has cleansed my soul;
I see rain falling to the thirsty ground
And know Thy life-giving love;
I see a thunderstorm,
And am aware of Thy vital force;
I look into a dear friend's face
And see Thy sweetness and beauty,
Thy compassion, calm strength,
Thy love for mankind.
I see these things, and my heart's one compelling desire
Is that others might see Thee in one
        other small place—
In me.

I WOULD GIVE THANKS for my God
To whom I can give my life
And so be as free from myself
As I will;
For my God who enables me
To have principles and integrity
In matters where, without His saving grace,
I might have none;
For my God whose mercy for me
Lets me give mercy and compassion to others;
For my God who made me a woman
Capable of loving deeply, fully, well
    and faithfully;
For my God who gave
The beloved Christ to hold me fast forever
While I search, seek, grope and rebel.
And I fall to my knees
In humility and surrender,
Knowing I am dear to Him.

God made me a woman

GOD MADE ME A WOMAN.
Why?
What would God have me do?
Woman gives a purpose to man;
Woman gives love;
Woman is a source of comfort and softness;
Woman is beauty in the eyes of those who love her;
Woman is gentle strength and truth to children;
Woman gives.
I would be nothing but woman,
But if I give, from whom shall I receive?
One Source supplies my needs—
He is my Purpose;
He gives me love in such abundance;
He is the Source of my comfort;
The beauty which is His is too great for my eyes to fully see;
His strength and truth for His child
Give me life.
How much more does He give—
How gladly I receive.

GOD HAS MINED ME like a base ore
And has lifted me up.
He has sifted and sorted,
Leaving only that which can be used.
He has melted me through trials,
Then in the tremendous glory of Him
Ridded me of all impurities.
He tempered me in the white heat of His might,
Making me malleable
That He might shape me with gentle love
And kindly hands.
He has made me an instrument to be used by Him—
May I sing like a fine blade,
May I cut through cleanly and sharply with truth,
May I let myself be used for peace and not for war,
May I shine brightly,
Resting in the hands of my Master.

DEAR GOD, You have been so generous in Your giving to
me.
You have given of Your love and forgiveness with an open
hand,
Asking nothing in return but my small self.
You have given to me such a bountiful supply
of talents and gifts—
A sound and intelligent mind,
A healthy body,
Physical agility and coordination,
Mental agility,
The capacity to love and to accept love,
The wisdom of learning not to regret but to forgive,
Children,
For a while a man to love and have knowledge of,
And then You gave Yourself and Your love
And claimed me for Your own.
To think upon this makes my heart go winging.
I know that such privileges demand responsibilities,
And I pray that I may always use the talents and gifts
Freely (as they are given),
Carefully (to not misuse them),
Humbly, gratefully, lovingly,
And always striving to use them for Thy glory.

Amen.

MAY THOSE WHO LOVE THEE, LORD,
Always be concerned for the
Problems, sufferings, anxieties
And emotions of others who are
Troubled in their minds, hearts and bodies.
May we stop sitting on our hands
While we wait for Thee to bring
To us others, whom we in turn
Would give back to Thee;
Rather, point us in the right direction
And send us out searching
To look for those we might bring to Thee.
Let us be small lights,
That others might not stumble
As they walk through dark shadows
On a rough and crooked path,
Seeking to reach the Great Light
At the end.
For if we truly love Thee,
We cannot rest
While others know and love Thee not.

96 🌹

O GOD,
There is a man that I would
I could bring to Thee
That he might be made whole.
So full of himself, so aware of his shortcomings,
Yet helpless to change.
His heart aches and his mind seethes
Trying to escape from himself.
May he fall before the power of Thy
    Spirit
And in falling lose the tight-fisted grip
He has on himself.
May his heart and mind be laid bare to receive Thee.
What a man he could be for Thee, O God,
If he would give all
That he might receive all!

                                        Amen.

This is my God

DEEPER THAN THE DEEPEST DEPTH known to man,
Higher than the very high heaven,
Stronger, more solid, fearsome and formidable
Than the greatest mountain,
More lovely and beautiful than man can know—
This is my God.

My God, whom I would serve well,
Giving my best though it is not enough;
Who surrounds me with His merciful care
Yet demands justice of and from me;
Whose glory makes me drunk and leaves me
Utterly humble and helpless before it;
Whose love for me, and those like me,
        and
The knowledge of it,
Give such joy as to cause pain;
Whose forgiveness is all-embracing;
Who sets me free while He holds me fast;
My God—whom I love before all else.

Do you know Him?
Do you love Him?
Do you want Him?

HUG NOT YOURSELF to yourself,
   lest you be crushed!
Rather open wide your arms
   to receive God.
To so open your arms leaves
   the heart exposed.
Stretch with your soul
Toward the high place,
Knowing you cannot reach it
   in this life.

Who is this God?—
   So lowly to come live in us;
   So high He rules over all and is
      afar off;
   So gracious in His mercy;
This God who cannot be
   contained,
No matter how we try to
Fit Him to our image.
He is in the very soul and heart
   of the one who seeks Him.
He is everything everywhere;
Surrounding without,
Abiding within,
Upholding, supporting.

Take joy in knowing you cannot change Him,
Have peace through His presence,
Know His love given full and complete in
   our Lord Christ.

HOW DO I FIND THEE, LORD?
Most excellent—
    just—
    exciting—
    challenging—
    majestic—
    responsive—
    frightening—
    deep—
    full—
    kind—
    loving—
    gracious—
    merciful—
    forgiving—
    truthful—
    mighty—
    tasteful—
    compassionate—
    promising—
    giving—
    receiving—
    righteous—
    blessed—
    needed—
    loved—
    sought—
    desired—
    vital and living—

Thou art all things, Lord,
And I find Thee good!

WHY CHOOSE SADNESS when there is joy?
Why choose tears when there is laughter?
Why choose anger when there is peace?
Why choose emptiness when there is fulfillment?
Why choose self-pity when there is self-understanding?
Why choose retreat when there is confrontation?
Why choose hurt when there is love?
Why choose ignorance when there is knowledge?
Why choose wrong when there is right?
Why choose to fall when there is strength to stand?
Why choose defeat when there is victory?
Why choose death when there is life?
Why choose fear when there is confidence?
Why choose ugliness when there is beauty?
Why choose silence when there is a voice to praise?
Why choose slavery when there is freedom?

Why choose nothing when there is all in Christ!

LONELY, tired and in utter despair
I knocked timidly at a door.
The door was swung open wide, and there
Was a room, so big, so warm and so bright.
No one was seen, no one asked who I was,
And yet I was accepted for what I was, and
Wrapped in a blanket of love, compassion and understanding.
I asked for a bite of bread and was fed a banquet.
I asked for a sip of water and was given a cup of life.
Then friends came, new and old, held out their hands
And they and the Presence unseen lifted me to my feet
    and held me until I could stand alone.
To stay in this room is all that I could ask,
And yet I know that I must go back out the door
And bring others to the warm and bright room
That is big enough to hold anyone who wants to come in.
I can go out again because I know the door is always open,
    and the room ready for me to live in, that it will always
    be there, and the knowledge of it will always draw
    me home—
After I've run the errands on which I've been sent.

II

THE VOICES
OF THE WORLD

II

Man has carved a trail

MAN has carved a trail,
   but at what price!

There a piece of human trash,
Discarded by another of his own kind
Who drained him of his energy
      and knowledge,
His drive and purpose,
And then tossed him aside:

A child whose heart and mind
      are torn
Because its home has been shattered
By adults seeking their own
      pleasure:

A family living in wretchedness,
Existing in cold or hot, filth
      and rags
While another lives fatly
   off their misery:

Nearby a man—of dark color,
   yet a man—
Whose right to the freedom
   and dignity
Of being
Has been denied by another
Out of fear:

A young man who lies and
    robs
And who sweats cold sweat
Because he has succumbed
To sweet-talking sellers of dope
    and booze.

Man has sold himself and his own kind—
For power, for money, for pleasure.
He feels no need for God
For he has other gods, including himself.
He has lost his soul
And neither knows nor cares.

Man has carved a trail,
    but at what price!

THE VOICE OF THE REBEL cries out
And is muffled
In the cotton of demands
For conformity, regularity, punctuality
        and general punctiliousness.
There is no place for him in the
Neat and ordered measured things
        of a conformist world . . . unless
        he already has
Power or money or position or
        reputation and renown.

The rebel must live and so sells
        his creativity
For the security of his children,
That they might have food and shelter—
Indeed, that he himself might have food
        and shelter.

The world says, "Speak to us," or
        "Sing to us,"
And then will not listen.
The world cannot stand for long the
        discomfort
Of the rebel, for he would upset
Their comfortable ways.
They make little room for him,
They do not allow for such individual
If such allowance can be prevented . . .
For he mocks much which they hold dear.

The voice of the rebel cries out
      and is
Muffled.

THIS MIGHTY COUNTRY CRIES.
It cries for God and knows Him not.
It invites Him and receives Him not.
It claims His blessing and denies His power.

How long, O Lord, will we turn
      from Thee—
How long wilt Thou yearn over us—
How long until we know Thee
In full awe-fulness and might!

We have sinned mightily before Thee:
      We have left in need those who are in need;
      We have left unloved those who need love;
      We have clutched to ourselves that which should
            be shared or cast away;
      We have closed our eyes to that which is unpleasant;
      We have plugged our ears to the cries from injustice,
            poverty, loneliness;
      We have stolen the bones beneath the table and left
            no thing.

We hide our faces from Thee, that Thou seest not our shame,
Yet our very souls are known to Thee.

Deliver us from ourselves,
That we might honor Thee honorably,
And be a song of gladness in Thy mouth!

OUR FATHER,

Cast not from Thee
A world sick of itself,
Yet unable to find its own way
Back to health;
Whose people find themselves
    inadequate
To keep pace within
With the numbers, the formulae,
    the things
That have pressed them so strongly
From without.
Inadequate, yet still looking
    to themselves
For an answer they cannot give.
Running, panting, striving
To run the race of the swift,
They fall exhausted by the way,
Wondering why they fell.
They do not rise to run again
But pass their lives by the side
    of the great road
And they watch as others fall,
Offering no help.

Wilt Thou spit out this lukewarm us?
Wilt Thou spit us out and be done,
Or leave us in our vacuum of pointless play
And small values?

Without Thee we are lost,
Yet how canst Thou speak to those
Who are lost but know it not?

Into the quiet sanctuary

INTO THE QUIET SANCTUARY I step.
The sanctuary—God's physical refuge
Where I may seek Him in His serenity,
Where He abides in calm and love
And lifts my heart from its bed
Of battles and temptations.
Here I feast at my Lord's table
And my starving spirit is fed.
Here my soul is replenished.
Here I hear God's Word—and often squirm,
For I fall so short of what He would have me be.
Here I bow my head and knee,
For God is here.

THANK YOU, GOD,
 For a house to live in,
 For a full stomach,
 For a warm bed,
 For good friends,
 For children and their innocence, trust and love;

 For green trees that shelter and shade,
 For the busy-ness of the day,
 For the quietness of the night,
 For music and books,
 For watching over us while we sleep,
 For guiding and forgiving.

For Christ do we thank You
 Most of all,
 For He is Your greatest gift of love.

         Amen.

DEAR FATHER, I would try to prepare myself now
To be worthy of the invitation to sit at Thy table,
To partake of bits of bread and sips of wine
That are a symbol of Thy body given for me
And others who have sinned.
There are tears in my eyes—
Of sadness that man, which You made in so
        wondrous a fashion,
Should cause You such grief and sacrifice
That You let Your own Son be crucified
For his poor sake;
Of joy, that You loved Your creation this much.
O Father, let me be crucified too—
If not on a cross of wood and
With nails hammered into my hands and feet
And a spear thrust into my side,
Then by the knowledge that I can never
Be worthy of such a sacrifice.
Give me the grace to lower my eyes
And bow my head in shame
For the sorrow that I and others like me
Must cause You.
And then, forgive me, I humbly pray.

                                    Amen.

DEAR LORD, for those who would try to serve and love
    Thee,
The image of the cross is very much present,
And the knowledge of the awful agony that was Yours—
The strained, flayed, taut muscles nailed down
To a tree;
The heart that would break because of
Mankind's self-made blindness to
The love, compassion and forgiveness
Sent as a gift from God through You.
Thou didst weep for us—
How many tears we should shed for ourselves
Because we are such fools!
And yet, there comes the knowing that,
While You suffered and died for us,
You did rise, and leave a grave sealed by a stone
Too heavy to move,
Showing Yourself in human form to man once more.
O Lord, to know that You love me this much,
That You would show me the power of eternal life
Over death on a cross,
And the blinding beautifulness of it,
How can I not kneel before You
And give You this life of mine now,
That I too may know the
Joy and anticipation of another life
To be lived forever with You
And in Your presence?

                                        Amen.

124 🌹

THE TIME of the Christ Child is near,
A cold time of year.
But my heart glows
And my soul is glad
For a God who came to me
In the life of a Child.

A new life—remember you Eternal Life
Was born that night!

I wonder—when God gave His gift—
Did He know it would be so rejected
        by so many?
He gave Himself in a love so great
That man can never fully comprehend it
        nor accept it all.

This tiny Babe, so small,
His life humbly, crudely, magnificently
        begun,
Who was to change man's life and his world,
This Child of God—

May I be very aware of Him as I
        celebrate
The anniversary of His coming—
For He lives still.

DEAR FATHER,
A year has almost spent itself,
Each person knowing it in his own way.
What has it brought me?
Sorrow, grief and loss,
A loneliness I had not known before,
And through these things a new awareness and love
Of Thee.
Thou hast greatly blessed me
And I give Thee thanks.

In the new year to come
Wilt Thou find me newly resolved
        To love Thee better,
        To seek Thy ways,
        To reflect Thy love in such a way
                as not to humiliate, abuse, or
                    hurt those about me by word or act,
        To leave myself open to receive Thee,
        To give my best in all I do.

I would ask Thee now to guide me through times
Not yet known to me
(For Thou only knowest what is to be),
That I might live the life Thou hast given me
Worthily of the gift.